Copyright 1989 Whitecap Books (Toronto) Ltd.
First published 1989 by Whitecap Books (Toronto) Ltd.
Suite 403—77 Mowat Avenue, Toronto, Ontario M6K 3E3

Book Design by Brad Nickason
Introduction by Michael Kluckner
Photo Editing by Brad Nickason
Edited by Elaine Jones

Third Printing, 1994

Canadian Cataloguing in Publication Data

Main entry under title:

Vancouver Island

ISBN 0-921396-16-3

1. Vancouver Island (B.C.) — Description and
travel — Views.

FC3844.4.V36   1989   971.1'34'00222
F1089.V3V36   1989   C89-091114-2

Printed and bound in Canada by Friesen Printers.

PHOTO CREDITS: **J.G. Brower**, pages 73, 96. **Michael E. Burch**, pages 6, 10, 11, 15, 18, 19, 21, 28-29, 32. **Albert Chin**, pages 44-45. **Janet Dwyer/First Light**, page 23. **Jeff Foot**, page 9. **Brad Hampson**, pages 16-17. **Al Harvey**, pages 30, 31, 56, 110, 112A. **Bob Herger**, pages 3, 8, 13, 14, 22, 33, 40, 42, 43, 46, 47, 48, 49, 50-51, 61B, 68, 70, 72, 75, 81, 82, 85, 93, 98-99, 100, 101, 104, 105, 106, 107, 108-9, 111, 112D. **Thomas Kitchin/First Light**, page 88. **Gary Lunny**, pages 5, 27, 37, 38-39, 83. **Colleen MacMillan**, page 59. **Rick Marotz**, page 71. **Vlado Matisic**, pages 12, 155. **G.E. Maurer**, page 112C. **David Nunuk/First Light**, pages 89, 90, 91, 92, 102. **Joyce Peck**, pages 24-25, 26, 35, 36, 54, 60, 61C 78, 79. **Michael Robertson**, pages 94-95. **Marin Petkov**, pages 34, 66, 69, 60, 77. **Steve Short**, pages 1, 52-53, 84, 86-87, 112B. **Steve Short/First Light**, front cover, page 4. **A.E. Sirulnikoff/First Light**, back cover, page 20. **Roy Stephens**, pages 57, 61A, 62, 63, 64-65, 67, 74, 76, 97, 103. **Peter Timmerman**, page 58. **Ron Watts/First Light**, page 41.

Preceding page: The big sky and splendid sweep of Qualicum Beach.

Opposite: One of B.C.'s large coastal ferries threads through the Gulf Islands between the mainland and Vancouver Island.

VANCOUVER ISLAND

Introduction by Michael Kluckner

Contents

Introduction

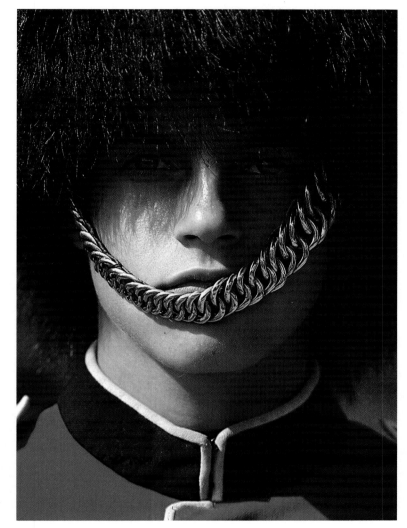

No generalization is possible about Vancouver Island, as it is both wet and dry, old-fashioned and brand new, sedate and raucous, gentle and rugged. There are almost as many different *types* of islanders as there are islanders. The climate and the vegetation change almost with each mile one travels. There are areas of untouched wilderness, near towns dominated by the smoking chimneys of heavy industry. But amidst all this diversity, there is a unifying factor: Vancouver Island itself, a verdant ship which, like islands everywhere, creates an "island mentality" in its residents. The "us" on the island are both fortunate to be there and economically disadvantaged by isolation; the "them" are the visitors and investors and potential settlers from the mainland.

Diverse it is. Victoria is one extreme: the "banana belt" of Canada, a genteel and sophisticated small city with a fascinating history, beautiful scenery, and a steady employer (the government, for it is the provincial capital). The west coast, most accessible around Ucluelet and Tofino and the Pacific Rim National Park, is another: a stunning habitat of surf and seals and eagles and untrammelled islands, at many times of the year almost lost in mist or drenched and buffeted by westerly squalls from the ocean. The Cowichan area on the east coast—"the warm land" of little farms and historic churches—is yet another. Elsewhere, Campbell River's salmon fishing attracts enthusiasts from around the world, and Strathcona Park has magnificent opportunities for recreation.

Not only is Vancouver Island distinctive for its landscapes and seascapes, and unusual for the diversity of its communities and the activities and lifestyles of its residents, but it also has an unusual and rather magical history which seems to cling to rock and tree, to church and farmhouse, and reminds the modern resident and visitor of the civilizations, both native and colonial, which occupied the island before our modern global village took possession. In that time before modern technology, Vancouver Island was truly isolated, and the native inhabitants—mainly Kwakiutl in the north, the Nootka on the west coast, and the Coast Salish in the southeast—developed a harmonious existence, with nature if not with each other. Their ability to harvest the bounty of the land and the sea—especially the latter—allowed them a comparatively luxurious life, and the freedom from privation to develop a complex and unique culture and art. Evidence of this native civilization and the natural world which supported it is everywhere: in the people themselves, and their rejuvenated spirit following more than a century of white settlement and their consequent domination, disease, and despair; in

Opposite: A sunset at Long Beach, on the west coast of Vancouver Island.

Above: Young busby'd guard in Victoria, a city sometimes said to be "more English than the English."

the sea and its creatures, including the killer whales, porpoise and fish of the west coast, and the clams and oysters of the intertidal shorelines of bays and inlets; in the cedars of the forests, which provided wood for their cooking fires, dwellings, canoes and (in the north) totem poles; on the meadows of the southeastern part of the island, in the springtime, grows the dark blue camass flower, which is the flag for the starchy bulb that was a major food item. Today, even those visitors who venture no further afield than Victoria can absorb some of the native culture in the splendid Royal British Columbia Museum, the adjoining Thunderbird Park, and the nearby museum and gallery commemorating the life and work of Emily Carr, a Victoria-born artist whose turn-of-the-century paintings of the rainforest and villages capture the gloomy grandeur of what was, in her day, the ruined remains of the Indian civilization.

Explorers from elsewhere, including Chinese, Japanese and Spanish, visited Vancouver Island, but none left any lasting imprint. One was Juan de Fuca, the namesake of the strait separating Vancouver Island from the Olympic peninsula of Washington State; he was a sailor, in the employ of the Spaniards who had colonized California, whose observations of the island, made during an expedition late in the sixteenth century, were the first recorded by a white man. Nearly two hundred years later, in 1778, the English Captain James Cook's search for a Northwest Passage led him up the west coast of North America, where he made a landfall on Nootka Island, not far from the modern community of Tahsis. Early in the 1790s, Captain George Vancouver explored and charted the area, but Great Britain's interests were elsewhere, occupied in Europe with the aftermath of the French Revolution and the rise of Napoleon.

The area remained interesting to traders, however. The Hudson's Bay Company, which dominated the fur trade in British North America, established a trading post in 1824 at Fort Vancouver, at the mouth of the Columbia River on the Washington-Oregon border. But it soon found that its ability to trade throughout the "Oregon Territory" was threatened by the western expansion of American settlers in their covered wagons on the Oregon Trail of storybook and western movie fame. The company looked to the north to locate a new trading post and fort on indisputably British territory, and in 1842 established Fort Victoria, named for the young queen who had ascended to the British throne a few years earlier. Seven years later, the Hudson's Bay Company received a charter from the British crown to administer and colonize Vancouver Island, for which it paid an annual rental of seven shillings.

Over the next few decades, Victoria and the neighbouring farming communities became colonized, mainly with émigrés from England. Even as early as the 1870s, the southern end of Vancouver Island was very different from the frontier settlements elsewhere in B.C. and western Canada. It offered a pleasant climate and a refined way of life; in short, the colonists were "more English than the English." As well, Vancouver Island became a magnet for retirees from the colonial civil service, the "old China hands," and tea planters from Ceylon, and for the famed "remittance men"—the second and subsequent sons of English gentry who, because of the custom of primogeniture, would not inherit any substantial portion of a family estate, and instead received a "remittance" and often a minor title which allowed them to live in style. Servants were plentiful, usually Chinese, and cheap (only $20 to $25 a month), freeing their well-educated employers for a graceful, formal life, and allowing them to indulge their penchant for politics. Many of the new residents brought enough capital from "home" (England) to build large houses on extensive grounds, and establish prosperous commercial operations—mainly in trade with Hawaii, San Francisco, and the outports up the coast. Another source of business was in supplying the gold-diggers who

swarmed into the trackless British Columbia interior in the late 1850s, and later settled in the city of New Westminster—the capital of the new mainland colony of British Columbia. In 1866, the two colonies amalgamated, although the capital stayed at the much more populous, better-established Victoria.

The promise of a railway—the ultimate solution to the age-old lack of a Northwest Passage—lured British Columbia in 1871 into Confederation with far-away, infant Canada (the prairies separating British Columbia with eastern Canada were sparsely settled and had been controlled until 1869 by the Hudson's Bay Company). Victoria was named as its western terminus, ensuring continuing prosperity for Vancouver Island. However, when that promise collapsed in 1884, and the new city of Vancouver was created as the terminus, resentment increased between islanders and mainlanders. Many of the settlers who arrived in New Westminster and the Cariboo gold towns were from Ontario and the Maritimes, and were Canadian, "small town," and "middle class" in their attitudes compared with the sophisticated English colonial spirit which permeated Vancouver Island. Joseph Pemberton, an aristocratic Anglo-Irishman who owned a 1,200-acre farm in what is now the Oak Bay suburb of Victoria, summed up the old-time islanders' feelings: "True loyalty's to Motherland / And not to Canada / The love we bear is second-hand / To any step-mama."

Beginning in the 1850s, settlers began to move north from the Victoria area and found splendid farmland in the lee of the mountains along the gulf, eventually founding communities including Cowichan, Chemainus, Parksville and Courtenay. A tremendous amount of development began in the Nanaimo area, and extended gradually to include communities such as Wellington and Ladysmith, because of the huge quantities of coal found there. Initially it was the Hudson's Bay Company which mined it and delivered it to a ready market at the Royal Navy's Esquimalt station near Victoria. One mine manager named Robert Dunsmuir found an especially rich seam near Departure Bay, and soon came to dominate the coal market and, to a great extent, the entire economy of Vancouver Island. Dunsmuir became the kingpin in a syndicate which built the Esquimalt & Nanaimo railway, connecting the coalfields with the population; his wealth built him the extraordinary "Craigdarroch" castle in Victoria, and built his son James the even more splendid "Hatley Park" at Royal Roads. But the relationship between Nanaimo and Victoria in the heyday of coal was rather like a fairytale of an ugly stepdaughter and a cruel stepmother: a lot of Victoria's grace and elegance was due to the prosperity made possible by the Dunsmuirs' collieries in the Nanaimo area; the rise of a militant and disaffected working class, which struck and rioted repeatedly in the years before coal declined due to the invention of oil-powered technology, came about because of the black poverty and dangerous conditions in which most of the workers lived and toiled.

The lumber industry on the island developed early in the history of the colony. William Banfield (remembered, though misspelt, in the little westcoast town of Bamfield) investigated the possibilities of logging around Barkley Sound in the 1850s; Captain Edward Stamp started a sawmill at Port Alberni in 1857, several years before he began the more enduring Hastings Sawmill at the future site of Vancouver. The first pulp mill started operations in the 1890s on the Somass River near Alberni. Port Alice is a pulp and paper company town founded

---

Opposite: At the foot of Government Street, Victoria's wide causeway borders the Inner Harbour. Artists, Scots bagpipers and other musicians play and paint year round on the broad sidewalk.

around the end of the First World War; another pulp mill operated briefly nearby at Alert Bay.

Many of the little towns ringing Vancouver Island have survived some years with fishing, others with logging, others with mining, as the need for raw materials fluctuated, for always Vancouver Island has been isolated, and its economy has either boomed or busted. Tourism has been a stabilizing factor in the island's economy since the turn of the century: originally, there was the lavish scheme to attract the Canadian Pacific Railway's well-heeled world travellers to Victoria with the construction of the Empress Hotel; in the 1920s, brochures describing the island's fine climate lured tourists made mobile by the newly invented motorcar. By the end of the First World War, visitors were able to drive the Island Highway from Victoria through Nanaimo to Campbell River, or cross the island from Parksville to Port Alberni on the new Canadian Highway. An even newer breed of tourists, that joins with the residents in the appreciation and protection of the natural wonders of the west coast, has been a feature of Vancouver Island since the 1970s.

When I think of Vancouver Island, a number of very different images come to mind. Firstly, I think of the soft, pastoral landscape of the Saanich Peninsula just north of Victoria and in the Duncan-Cowichan-Mill Bay area, with its hedgerows and long views across the Strait of Georgia to Mount Baker. Then, I think of Victoria itself and the rocky, picturesque landscape marked out with stone walls and the rather vertical, shingle covered wooden houses of the late Victorian period, the lawns studded with garry oaks; in February, I see on the rambling, craggy, informal gardens of some of the old estates the wild daffodils and magical purple satin flowers which carpet the grass with drifts of shy colour. And, finally, when I think of Vancouver Island, I think of a summer around 1970 I spent on a salmon troller based in Ucluelet, before the Pacific Rim National Park was established and the road from Port Alberni was paved and improved, at a time when getting to Ucluelet or Tofino was best done by sea. That summer, we fished the grand bank off the coast for several days at a stretch, interspersed with almost endless walks along deserted Long Beach with the surf crashing in, the scrubby shore pines swept back and away from the ocean winds like stiff, unwashed hair; we walked past the squatter's driftwood shacks, smelling the fish cooking over their campfires. Out on the boat, at dawn, we awoke to a world all sil-

very grey and silent, rolled on the quicksilver ocean swell, counted the birds in the enormous sky and watched the whales and seals while waiting for the morning's salmon run.

It is still like that there.

Opposite: Sometimes violent, sometimes serene, the moody grandeur of Long Beach on the island's wild west coast lives on in those who have stood on this shore.

Above: An orca, or killer whale, shows its distinctive fin. Regular whale watching trips now give tourists from around the world a chance to see whales in the wild.

The South Island

The southern tip of Vancouver Island is dominated by Victoria, capital city of British Columbia and a charming garden city surrounded on three sides by the sea. Thanks to the warm offshore current and its protected position, Victoria has moderate temperatures year-round. Not surprisingly, the city is famed for its flower displays, particularly the hanging baskets in the downtown area.

The natural beauty of Victoria has made the city a popular destination for visitors, and there is no lack of things to do or see. The city core centres around Victoria Harbour, where working vessels such as fishboats, freighters, ocean liners and ferries share the water with yachts and other pleasure craft. Overlooking the Inner Harbour are the stately Empress Hotel, built in 1908 as part of the CPR chain of grand hotels, and the Victorian-style B.C. Legislative Buildings, completed in 1897. Together they present an imposing and beautiful front, surrounded by wide green lawns and brilliant flower beds. One of the standbys of any visit to Victoria, afternoon tea is served at the Empress in high fashion.

The city has retained much of the scale of a century ago, and quaint shops, housed in turn-of-the-century buildings, have been renovated to carefully preserve the "old-English" feel of the city, enhanced by double-decker buses and horse-drawn carriages. Surrounding residential neighbourhoods contribute to the charm of Victoria, boasting many fine examples of Victorian- and Edwardian-era homes. At the same time, Victoria has a decidedly modern aspect; shops carry up-to-the-minute fashions as well as tweed skirts and brogues, a multitude of restaurants cater to every taste, and music, art and theatre flourish.

Near Victoria, within a day's drive of the city, there are many areas of scenic and historic interest. West from Victoria, Highway 14 follows along Juan de Fuca Strait. It passes through the small communities of Sooke and Jordan River, skirts a number of beaches, and ends at the logging community of Port Renfrew. Past Sooke the feeling of the countryside changes, as the road leaves the more protected eastern side of the island and the influence of the open Pacific Ocean begins to be felt. Heavy ocean swells roll into shore, polishing beach pebbles to a rounded smoothness, and impressive storms can sweep down Juan de Fuca Strait.

Just a short distance from Port Renfrew is Botanical

Opposite: The Olde English Inn in Esquimalt, one of Victoria's original residential areas. On the grounds is an exact replica of Anne Hathaway's cottage.

Above: A statue of Queen Victoria overlooks her namesake city, the province's capital. The turn-of-the-century Legislative Buildings, which still house the provincial legislature, can be seen in the background.

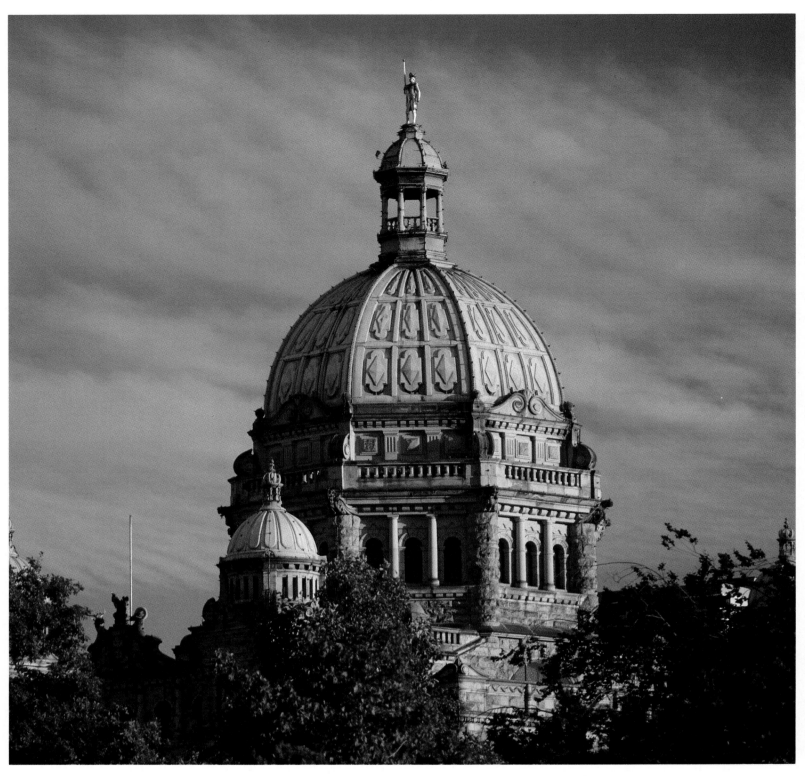

Bay, which has been a marine explorer's delight since it was discovered in 1901. A wide sandstone shelf has been sculpted into deep pools and caves by the surf; at low tide a multitude of intertidal life forms can be seen, many of which are normally only found below the tide line.

On the Saanich Peninsula, the biggest attraction is Butchart Gardens, located at Brentwood Bay. The original garden, begun in 1904 by Jennie Butchart, was created to hide the scars of a limestone quarry. It has since grown to cover some 130 acres (52 hectares). Trees, shrubs, lawns and hundreds of varieties of flowers combine in a profusion of colour and brilliant garden design that attracts visitors from around the world.

Elsewhere on the Saanich Peninsula, there are many delightful coves and bays to explore, as well as hiking, fishing, and swimming and boating in local lakes. At the tip is Swartz Bay, with ferries to Tsawwassen on the mainland and the adjacent Gulf Islands. At the southern end of the

Peninsula is Goldstream Provincial Park, once the site of the island's first sawmill, the scene of a brief gold strike, and now an attraction during the annual salmon spawning run. From here the excellent Island Highway begins its climb up Malahat Mountain and continues along the east coast.

Above: A gilded statue of Captain Cook, first European visitor to Vancouver Island, stands atop the copper dome of Victoria's Legislative Buildings.

Opposite: The ivy-clad walls of the Empress Hotel form a backdrop to the capital city's famous hanging baskets. Built just after the turn of the century, in Victoria's golden age, the Empress rivalled Europe's grand hotels. The old English street lamps in the city's downtown core are decked out with a profusion of flowers five months of the year.

Opposite: Restoration of the city's century-old heritage buildings began here, in Bastion Square, near the northeast side of the harbour in the late 1960s. The city has since devoted much time and attention to restoring and preserving the architecture of its turn-of-the-century affluence.

Above: The four-storey fairytale architecture of Craigdarroch Castle was commissioned in the late 1880s by B.C.'s richest man, coal baron Robert Dunsmuir, as a present for his wife.

Preceding pages: A fountain graces the gardens of Beacon Hill Park, a 150-acre (60 ha) landmark in Victoria, established in the 1850s.

Above: Considered the handsomest house in Canada before World War I, and today home to Royal Roads Military College, Hatley Castle was built by James Dunsmuir, son of Robert, on the proceeds from the Dunsmuir family's vast coal, lumbering and shipping empire.

Opposite: One of the covered walkways of Hatley Castle's Botanical Gardens. The gardens, comprising formal and informal, Japanese, Italian and English styles are open daily to the public.

Opposite: The Italianate design, mansard roof and huge clock of Victoria's City Hall, opened in 1878, punctuates busy Douglas Street. Behind lies the beautifully restored McPherson Playhouse.

Above: Just outside Victoria, Fable Cottage's extraordinary architecture and themed floral gardens attract many curious visitors.

Opposite: Native Victorians' childhood memories often include an unforgettable first encounter with the power of west coast Indian art among the totems of Thunderbird Park, adjacent to the Royal British Columbia Museum. Today, native Indian carvers can often be seen at work on new totems in an open studio shed nearby.

Above: A kilted piper plays beside a totem pole near the Empress Hotel, entertaining strollers in the Inner Harbour.

Preceding pages: Victoria's Legislative Buildings are illuminated nightly by thousands of bulbs.

Above: A sailboat plys the waters of Oak Bay.

Opposite: Narrow Fan Tan Alley in Chinatown, once home to fan-tan gambling clubs, now features shops and restaurants.

Above: The Royal British Columbia Museum has an international reputation as one of the country's most exciting and innovative museums. Visitors of all ages can wander the streets of a meticulously re-created pioneer town and experience the sights and sounds of a Kwakiutl longhouse. The "Open Ocean" exhibit, the Museum's latest *tour de force*, simulates a journey in a "nautilus" submarine into the little-known depths of the ocean.

Opposite: The Maritime Museum on Bastion Square covers coastal shipping, naval and fishing history. Also housed here is the *Tillicum*, a dugout canoe paddled by a man called Voss across the Pacific Ocean in 1901.

Above: The *Princess Marguerite*'s Union Jack funnels are a familiar sight in Victoria's harbour: the "old lady" plies the waters daily between Victoria and Seattle, Washington. Beside her is one of the Black Ball ferries, which run between Victoria and Port Angeles, Washington.

Opposite: Night, and the *Pacific Princess*, one of the many cruise ships which visit the city in the summer months, slips away from its day's moorage at Ogden Point.

Opposite: Fisgard Light and the pre-World War I defence battery at Fort Rodd Hill together speak of the coast's vulnerability to attack and of its treacherousness to passing ships.

Above: Members of the Victoria Golf Club enjoy one of the world's most scenic links—and lose a lot of balls to the ocean. Local legend supported by occasional sightings insists that this particular stretch is haunted by the restless ghost of a woman murdered by her husband early in the century.

Following pages: Victoria's annual Swiftsure Classic yacht race attracts over 400 participants who compete in two world class events. Every year a week of festivities usher in this island tradition.

Above: Visitors to the Undersea Gardens on the Inner Habour can walk beneath the sea to view the aquarium's collection of local sea life in their outdoor pens.

Opposite: Once left to decay, Victoria's Old Town has been restored to its former charm. The Market Square area is now a vibrant shopping district.

Above: The 11-mile (18 km) stretch of Saanich Inlet is the southernmost of the many deep fjords which characterize the island's "wild broken coast."

Opposite: A meadow of wildflowers overlooks the Saanich Inlet, where the small ferry pictured runs north between Brentwood Bay and Mill Bay, saving motorists the drive over the Malahat.

Following pages: The now world-famous Butchart Gardens began as a hobby for the cement manufacturing pioneer Robert Butchart and his wife Jennie who, just over eighty years ago, wondered what could be made of an abandoned limestone quarry.

Above and opposite: Native plants mix with the rare and exotic in the Butchart Gardens on the Saanich Peninsula. The gardens are open to the public every day of the year.

Opposite: The "wilder shore"—the island's renowned and sparsely populated west coast—begins at Sooke.

Above: An aerial view of Sooke.

Following pages: French Beach Park, near Sooke. The breakers of the open Pacific tumble local beach stones to an extraordinary roundness and smoothness along the exposed coast.

The East Coast

The east coast of Vancouver Island, from the broad Cowichan Valley to Campbell River, has a special appeal. The pace seems to slow and the vastness of the land forms a backdrop to a series of small communities, rolling countryside dotted with pastoral farms, some excellent recreational areas, and seaside resorts. The best advice for a traveller is to take some time to explore; each stop has its own particular attractions.

Once over Malahat Mountain, with its spectacular views of the Saanich Peninsula and the distant mountains, the highway enters the Cowichan Valley. The Cowichan Valley is known for the fine fishing in the Cowichan River and for the handiwork of the Cowichan Indians, the largest band in B.C., whose unique handknit sweaters have become well known. The largest centre in the valley, Duncan, is on the highway, but those with a little time to spare can follow the meandering backroads between the coast and the Trans-Canada Highway. Picturesque bays and marinas, country churches and tiny villages are the reward, and a little further north, the tiny town of Chemainus is well worth the short detour from the highway. A sawmill town that was left without an economic base when the mill shut down, Chemainus has been revitalized by local artists who began painting murals depicting the history of the area on building walls. Each year the number of murals increases and the town's historic wooden buildings are restored, creating a burgeoning tourist industry.

Nanaimo is the second largest city on Vancouver Island and the hub of the central island, with ferry service to Horseshoe Bay on the mainland. An industrial-based city with a long and interesting history, Nanaimo has recently begun maximizing the scenic assets of its protected seaside location and refurbishing the historic buildings.

Near Parksville, the highway branches west to Port Alberni. On the way it passes Englishman River Falls Provincial Park, Cathedral Grove and the bustling market at Coombs, where goats feeding on a sod roof are a startling attraction, and the good food and bargain prices are reason enough to linger. Cathedral Grove in MacMillan Provincial Park, a stand of 800-year-old Douglas firs, affords a unique opportunity to see first-growth coastal forest. The park is well-named; dwarfed by these original forest giants there is a feeling of awe, and the forest itself seems hushed.

From Parksville to Courtenay, the highway follows

Preceding pages: The Island Highway (Hwy. 1 to Nanaimo, where it becomes Hwy. 19) now connects communities up and down the east coast of the island between Victoria and Port Hardy.

Above: Moonrise near Nanaimo.

Opposite: Fishing boats tie up for the night at Deep Bay.

closely along the shoreline, affording superb views of the water and distant mountains. Along this route, there are dozens of beaches, resorts and villages that blossom in the summer months. The shallow beach at Parksville is ideal for beachcombing or childish pursuits like building sand structures, exploring for marine life or paddling in shallow pools left by the tide and warmed by the sun. Nearby is Rathtrevor Provincial Park, one of the favourite family camping parks in B.C.

At Comox there is a Canadian Armed Forces base and a ferry terminus for ships to Powell River on the mainland. From nearby Courtenay skiers and hikers take off for the mountains of Strathcona Provincial Park, B.C.'s oldest park, established in 1911. Forbidden Plateau, in the park, and Mount Washington, just outside the park, are two favoured skiing areas.

Campbell River is also an access point for Strathcona, but its main attraction is the chance to catch some of the salmon in the waters of Discovery Passage. The town has built a small industry on the success of visiting fishermen—with local hotels, motels, recreation areas, fishing guides and a variety of restaurants. Located about half-way up the island, Campbell River marks the transition to the northern part of the island.

Above: This quiet sweep of beach near Ladysmith invites exploration.

Opposite: Cows recline in a misty Cowichan Valley sunrise. Dairy farming is of considerable importance in the south of the island.

Opposite: The clear waters of picturesque Maple Bay harbour a marine life sanctuary that attracts scuba divers and underwater photographers year-round.

Above: Visitors to the 100-acre (40 ha) Forest Museum near Duncan thrill to the chance to ride a narrow-gauge logging train pulled by a working steam engine. The museum's indoor and outdoor exhibits focus on the evolution of the logging and lumber industry in the province.

Above: Chemainus, known locally as "the little town that did," successfully stabilized its economy by diversification, supplementing its pulp industry with tourism. A spacious horse-drawn carriage here awaits passengers for a tour of the town.

Opposite: Central to Chemainus's widely publicized urban revitalization scheme—awarded first prize in a 1983 New York-based competition—are its boisterous larger-than-life murals depicting local life and history, painted by local artists.

Above: Nanaimo, the industrial hub of the island, somewhat prophetically took its name from the Indian Snenymo, or "where the big tribe dwells." The sea plane terminal pictured here is only minutes from downtown.

Opposite: Dating from 1852, Nanaimo's Hudson's Bay Company-built bastion recalls the company town's past. By 1892, there were ten coal mines in the area and coal was being shipped as far south as California.

Preceding pages: Day dawns over Nanaimo. The ocean's ever-present and ever-changing face puts the town's busy industry into perspective.

Above: This sweep of sandy beach at Parksville, only a couple of hours from Vancouver or Victoria, is a magnet to city-worn natives and tourists alike.

Opposite: Royal Canadian Navy vessels on an exercise in Nanoose Bay.

Above: Goats roam the roof of the Coombs market, inland from Qualicum Beach, a popular stop on the road to Long Beach.

Opposite: According to local legend, Englishman River was named a century ago by Indians who discovered a white man's skeletal remains along its banks. Now the centrepiece of a large provincial park, the river provides refreshing fresh water swimming and a change from the beach in the summer.

Opposite: Awe-inspiring Cathedral Grove has preserved a stand of original growth trees. Visitors to the primeval grove can see towering Douglas-firs which predate the birth of Genghis Khan, and were already hundreds of years old before Columbus set foot in America.

Above: Sproat Lake is noted for its cutthroat and rainbow trout and for its enormous fire-fighting planes, the Martin Mars water bombers.

Above: Port Alberni is home to the largest forest products complex on the island, producing pulp, paper, shingles, plywood and lumber from several mills.

Opposite: A happy day's end. Sports fishermen flock from around the world, lured by such dream catches as this 74-pound (33 kg) salmon.

Opposite: Little Qualicum Falls challenge local teenagers to daring summer sports.

Above: Qualicum Beach, where the tide goes out a full mile (1.6 km), warming itself over the sand as it returns, has long been the watering hole of the island's wealthy.

Above: The verdant and fertile Comox Valley has drawn admiring remarks from visitors since an early survey vessel captain reported, "The extent and beauty of what we saw quite surprised us, and we agreed that this was the most promising spot for an agriculture settlement we have yet seen on the Island."

Opposite: A totem in Courtenay, in the Comox Valley. Historically, the valley was inhabited by the Komuckaway tribe whose name, meaning "abundance," still aptly describes the area.

Opposite: Winter in the populous south and east regions of Vancouver Island is normally gentle. But skiers need not go far to find higher and snowier elevations. Mt. Washington is a favourite ski resort mid-island, just outside Strathcona Provincial Park.

Above: Vancouver Island has been described as one big mountain chain relieved by plateaus and coastal flatlands. Here, a little leg work provides the hiker with spectacular views of Mt. Arrowsmith.

Above: Strathcona Provincial Park provides half a million acres (231,000 ha) of canoeing, kayaking, hiking and cross-country skiing, dominated by the snow-covered peaks of the island's highest mountains.

Opposite: Sunset at Fisherman's Wharf in Campbell River, one of the world's most renowned salmon fishing areas, attracting hopeful sports fishermen from all over North America, Europe and the Far East. Here, in the summer months, lines often tangle as dozens of boats jockey for position above a popular "hole" and experienced guides are worth their weight in trophy fish.

The North Island

At Campbell River, the terrain and the atmosphere begin to change and take on a distinctly northern character. The cozy signs of human habitation are fewer and the forests seem denser as the highway leaves the open coast. Inroads, primarily logging, have been made into the wilderness, but the north island still retains a pioneer feeling; the towns are less prettified, the surrounding forest less tamed, the climate less gentle. The landscape takes on a rugged, solitary beauty.

Tourism is just beginning to become a factor here, as appreciation for wilderness areas increases and access is improved, but logging is still the most important element in the north island economy. Past Campbell River, there is a noticeable increase in the numbers of logging trucks and heavy machinery on the road. Most of the larger communities here—Gold River, Port McNeill, Port Hardy and Port Alice—are based on the forestry industry, and the paved North Island Highway that now links these communities was until relatively recently a series of rough gravel roads. The countryside is honeycombed with logging roads that lead to remote areas.

Gold River is reached via the highway from Campbell River through Strathcona Provincial Park. Strathcona is B.C.'s largest park, at half a million acres (231,000 hectares), and it encompasses the highest peaks on the island and some of the grandest scenery in B.C., including Della Falls—at a spectacular 1,450 feet (440 m) Canada's highest waterfall. Three nature conservancy areas, where all motorized vehicles are banned, preserve the mountain habitats for hikers, canoers and kayakers. From Gold River, it's possible to take a day cruise to Friendly Cove, the historic site where Captain Cook first landed in 1778.

The village of Alert Bay, on Cormorant Island, is a short ferry trip from Port McNeill. An early salmon cannery location, Alert Bay is a mixed white and native village that is the home of the Nimpkish Indian Band. The village stands as a testament to the native culture: totem poles are an imposing presence throughout the village and a short distance from the ferry the U'Mista Cultural Centre and the Kwakiutl Big House display fine examples of native art.

Just southeast of Port McNeill is the tiny, picturesque village of Telegraph Cove. Originally a telegraph station and the location of a small milling operation, the cove saw duty by the Air Force during World War II. But the mainstay of village economy in the summer is now the annual influx of tourists that pass through on their way to the

Above: Hopeful until last light, these sports fishermen linger in the sunset.

Opposite: A huge fallen tree makes a broad path for hikers near Nimpkish.

killer whale grounds in nearby Robson Bight. The whales attract campers, naturalists and the merely curious, and whale-watching tours are offered out of Telegraph Cove.

Port Hardy, the largest northern community, is where the paved highway ends. From here, B.C. Ferries operates a service to Prince Rupert—a 15-hour cruise that travels the scenic Inside Passage.

At the northwest tip of the island is Cape Scott Provincial Park, 38,000 acres (15,000 hectares) of rugged wilderness accessed by a gravel road from Port Hardy. The area was settled by intrepid Danes in 1897, but the rigours of the climate and isolation doomed the community. Remnants of their settlement can still be seen today and their original wagon roads are part of the trail system in the park. For the truly adventurous, Cape Scott offers miles of untouched beaches fronting on the open Pacific and a forest wilderness that in some way exemplifies the north island—harsh, beautiful and untamed.

Above: Fishboats tie up at a Port McNeill wharf.

Opposite: The network of logging roads over the island's north end offer easy access to wilderness areas. Here campers prepare for a night near Beaver Cove.

Preceding pages: The picturesque Bunsby Islands were the site of the successful re-introduction of the nearly extinct sea otter in the 1970s.

Above: Whale-watching off the east coast of northern Vancouver Island is a popular attraction for tourists and residents alike.

Opposite: The gill nets of commercial fishermen dry on the wharf at Sointula, a town on Malcolm Island.

Above: Alert Bay on Cormorant Island is a short ferry ride from Port McNeill. The island is the centre of the Kwakiutl Nation and has a new museum of native Indian culture.

Opposite: Visitors to Alert Bay have a rare chance to see totems in their original setting.

Opposite: A float plane shares moorage with pleasure boats on Muchalat Inlet near Gold River.

Above: Remote Telegraph Cove just south of Alert Bay is a busy log booming area. Whale-watching expeditions also use the harbour as a home base.

Preceding pages: The light at Nootka warns ships away from "Graveyard of the Pacific," where between 1803 and 1979, there were 240 recorded shipwrecks.

Opposite: Sunset in the remote community of Rivers Inlet, an area famed among sports fishermen for its giant salmon.

Above: Just south of Cape Scott at the northwest tip of the island and accessible only by water or on foot from Holberg, Guise Bay and its neighbouring beaches are among the most spectacular in the world.

The West Coast

The west coast of the island has a very special magic. Swollen with the force of the open ocean, waves break ceaselessly on the long beaches and rocky headlands. The weather here varies from sunny skies of the purest wind-washed blue to mists that roll in and cling for days and winter storms of a terrifying fury. Here nature is at its most beautiful and powerful, creating vast land and seascapes that dwarf the tiny communities clinging to protected coves and bays.

The biggest draw for many visitors is Long Beach, part of Pacific Rim National Park. A spectacular stretch of sandy beach broken by rocky outcroppings, it runs some 19 miles (30 km) from Cox Point to Wya Point. Visitors can walk for hours along the hardpacked sand searching for treasures thrown up in the sand, explore for marine life in pools left by the tide in rocky outcroppings, visit the excellent information centre, or hike the trails carved out of the unique coastal forest. Demand for park campsites is high, and a number of private campgrounds and other accommodations have proliferated in the area.

Tofino, just north of Long Beach, and Ucluelet, some 25 miles to the south, are picturesque fishing villages that are also supply centres for Long Beach and the surrounding areas. The west coast is the scene of the annual gray whale migration each spring, when the gray whales travel from their breeding grounds at Baja California to the summer feeding grounds in the Bering Sea. From February until

May, avid naturalists and others who are simply fascinated with these giant mammals gather here to observe their passage. Both Tofino and Ucluelet offer whale watching tours at these times and throughout the summer months, when "resident" killer whales can be seen. From Tofino there are also opportunities to travel to Hot Springs Cove, Vancouver Island's only natural hot springs, 18 miles (29 km) up the coast, for a relaxing dip in the steaming pools.

Ucluelet sits at the upper edge of Barkley Sound, and Bamfield at the lower end. Cupped in the middle of the sound is an archipelago of some 100 islands and islets called the Broken Group Islands, now part of Pacific Rim National Park. The closely grouped islands form a maze of waterways that are mirror calm on the protected inner channels, while the outer islands take the full brunt of the

Preceding pages: Sunset at White Cliff Island in Queen Charlotte Strait.

Opposite: Steller's and California sea lions are common from the Saanich Peninsula north to the top of the island. "Hauling out" to bask in the sun is a favourite activity.

Above: A totem pole near Tofino. One of the coast's first peoples, the Nootka Indians have inhabited the area around Tofino for over 5,000 years.

open Pacific storms. The area is a wilderness paradise for canoeists, kayakers and sailboaters, with an abundance of wildlife, from sea lions to tufted puffins and, of course, the ever-present eagles, kingfishers and crows.

Off Barkley Sound, the Alberni Inlet almost bisects Vancouver Island. At its head is Port Alberni, since 1860, when the first sawmill for export lumber was established, a centre of logging and pulp mill operations. More recently it has become a base for tourism and commercial and sports fishing in the excellent waters of the inlet. The supply ship *Lady Rose* is based in Port Alberni. From here the vessel services fishing and logging camps, stopping at Bamfield and Ucluelet, and dropping off campers and their craft in the Broken Group Islands.

Bamfield is the head of the West Coast Trail, the third component of Pacific Rim National Park. This rugged trail is not for Sunday walkers; hikers must be prepared to take up to six days to get to the southern end of the trail at Port Renfrew. The trail was carved out of the forest as a lifesaving trail for survivors of ships that went down in the "Graveyard of the Pacific," as this southwest edge of the island was known. Today it is a popular destination for wilderness buffs who challenge the rigours of the trail for the rewards afforded by the incredible natural beauty.

Opposite: The Broken Group Islands, Barkley Sound.

Above: Docks near the charming fishing village of Tofino, just outside the Pacific Rim National Park.

Above: Tofino, looking towards Meares Island. Meares Island has lately been the site of a hard-fought battle by environmentalists and native Indians to save its ecologically sensitive forests, sacred to the Indians, from clear-cut logging.

Opposite: Giants are bred in the ideal conditions of the coastal rain forest where they are watered by up to three hundred inches (760 cm) of rain a year. Trees can grow to twelve feet (3.6 m) in diameter and over 300 feet (90 m) in height. Some trees on the island are thought to have begun life before the 7th century A.D.

Top left: A wall-size mural by Jan Vriesen in the new museum at Wickaninnish in the Pacific Rim National Park. **Top right:** Named after a famous Clayoquot chief, the surf of Wickaninnish Bay pounds the "singing sands" of Long Beach. **Bottom left:** The M.V. *Lady Rose*, a coastal supply ship, stops to drop kayakers at the Broken Islands; other tourists enjoy a round-trip sightseeing expedition. **Bottom right:** Hikers from all parts of the world enjoy the challenge of the turn-of-the-century maritime lifesaving trail between Bamfield and Port Renfrew.

Opposite: Experiencing the power of the Long Beach surf. Spray from winter breakers can be flung over a hundred feet (30 m) in the air.

Preceding pages: Sunset on Long Beach, and a glimpse of the tangle of logs piled high from years of violent winter storms.

Above and opposite: The old but still thriving fishing village of Ucluelet, which lies at the southern end of the Pacific Rim National Park, is "paradise" to some of its transplanted residents.